THE MARRIAGE TALK

THE MARRIAGE TALK

CARMEN WILDE

CONTENTS

Introduction

Discussing marriage can be nerve-wracking. Deciding when and how to have the marriage talk can lead to a lot of hesitation for many couples. However, having an open and honest conversation about the future of your relationship, which is essentially what the marriage talk is, can significantly enhance both the stability of your relationship and the depth of your love.

Engaging in the marriage talk allows you to understand more about yourself, your partner, and the unique bond you share. The biggest challenge you may face is learning to appreciate the outcome, no matter what it might be. In love, there are no winners or losers; the focus should be on mutual growth and understanding.

Before initiating this crucial conversation, make sure you approach it with an open heart. It's important not to let the fear of uncertainty weigh you down. Trust in yourself and your partner to navigate this talk together, with kindness and genuine honesty, so that you both feel heard and valued in love.

The marriage talk, when approached thoughtfully, should be a relaxed conversation that helps both partners set clear relationship goals. This practice enhances communication and maintains emotional closeness. Both partners should feel at ease bringing up the topic and discussing it without the pressure of expecting any specific outcome. Ultimately, the marriage talk is a refined way to address the most important question you will ever ask: "Do you have the courage to build a life with me?"

The only mistake you can make is to avoid asking the question in the first place. Embrace the courage to have this conversation, and let it strengthen the foundation of your relationship.

CHAPTER 1

Understanding the Importance of the Marriage Talk

Healthy romantic relationships thrive on the foundation of continuous and open communication. Regularly checking in on the state and direction of the relationship is an essential practice for every couple. These periodic "check-ins" help prevent misunderstandings and ensure both partners feel valued and heard, especially when it comes to important topics like marriage. By openly discussing the future, couples can avoid the common pitfall of misaligned values, where one partner may undervalue something significant, while the other overvalues their contributions.

There is often a misconception that discussing marriage too openly can feel unromantic or set a rigid precedent. However, this stereotype can actually undermine the benefits of honest and transparent communication. When couples openly talk about their long-term commitment and future together, they are, in fact, establishing a feedback-friendly environment. This proactive approach emphasizes the importance of healthy communication and reassures both partners of their mutual dedication.

By addressing marriage in a thoughtful and open manner, the conversation gains depth and meaning. Rather than feeling forced or unromantic, these discussions can enhance the romantic connection between partners. Talking about the future in this way serves to strengthen the relationship, fostering a shared vision and reinforcing the commitment to build a life together.

CHAPTER 2

Preparing for the Marriage Talk

Entering into a marriage talk requires careful preparation. First, you need to understand what you want from the conversation. Reflect on your relationship and your future goals together. It's crucial to have a clear idea of your beliefs, personal motivations, and standards. The following questions will help you clarify your position on engagement and marriage. This section is designed to help you focus on what is important to you in a relationship and evaluate where you currently stand.

Once you've reflected on what you want from the marriage talk, it's time to prepare for the actual conversation. Let's start by choosing the appropriate time and place for "the talk." A private, relaxed setting, such as a quiet café or your home, can be ideal. Afternoon or early evening is often the best time, as people tend to be tired, cranky, or rushed in the morning, especially on workdays. Avoid initiating the conversation immediately when your partner walks in the door or during high-stress situations.

Reflecting on Your Relationship

Take time to reflect on your journey as a couple. If you have been together for a while, consider how much you have changed individually and how you have grown together. Reflect on the experiences you've shared and the values that have held you together. Are these values still important?

People and relationships evolve over time. How have you both grown? Understanding your dreams, values, interests, and passions is essential. Don't undermine your likes, dislikes, opinions, dreams, thoughts, creativity, etc. These elements are vital for maintaining a strong sense of self, which is crucial for healthy self-esteem.

Does your partner share your values and aspirations? Do they possess qualities and experiences that align with the goals you wish to achieve together? Understanding how you have grown individually and what you share as a couple is critical. If you feel uncertain, seeking guidance from a therapist can be helpful. Remember, these questions and reflections are ongoing processes, not one-time discussions.

Does your partner appreciate you for who you are? Do you feel supported in your dreams? Is there a sense of equality in your activities and well-being? A good lifelong partner possesses qualities of a true friend—someone who appreciates and accepts you no matter what happens.

Setting the Right Environment

1. **Timing:** The first thing to consider is the timing of the talk. Schedule a time when you know you'll have privacy and won't be preoccupied with other worries. Avoid planning the conversation when your partner has a lot on their mind. Choosing a time when you both can talk without interruptions is crucial. This shows that you value the conversation and want your partner to feel comfortable.

2. **Privacy:** Ensuring privacy is essential for an open and honest conversation. Choose a setting where both of you will feel

comfortable speaking freely, such as a cozy café or a quiet spot at home. Many people opt for a relaxed meal at a local restaurant to help set the tone for a meaningful discussion.

3. **Remove Distractions:** Make sure there are no distractions around. If you're at home, turn off the TV, silence your phone, and create a calming atmosphere. Inform anyone who might interrupt you, such as housemates or neighbors, to avoid disturbances. This focus demonstrates that you are fully present and committed to the conversation.

CHAPTER 3

Key Components of the Marriage Talk

When it comes to the marriage talk, discussing your wants, needs, fears, and expectations is crucial. This conversation helps determine if both partners share the same vision for the future. Emotions can run high because there's a lot at stake. Some might think avoiding certain topics makes the talk easier or reduces conflict, but addressing all these questions is essential for a healthy and fulfilling marriage. Both partners deserve the chance to make informed decisions about what happens next.

Sharing these key components strengthens the foundation of your relationship and gives each partner the opportunity to make decisions that are mutually beneficial. After discussing individual components, defining the shared values and goals you both bring to the table is key. What do each of these elements contribute together? What shared values have you established, and what collaborative solutions are at the root of these values? How do your coping strategies complement each other, and how can you use these skills to support one another? How do your conflict resolution styles shape your relationship? What are some common goals you both have?

Shared Values and Goals

Dating is essentially an activity centered on the pursuit of shared values and future goals. Establishing baseline values and goals is a critical step before making further commitments. Without the "shared future" element, dating can feel like a hobby. That's why understanding the present values and goals of both parties is crucial.

When dating prospects recognize conflicting values or goals, it may be a sign that the relationship should not continue. The real effort should be to find someone whose values and goals align with yours, making the personal investment worthwhile. Addressing these potential issues early can prevent future conflicts and allow both partners to pursue a shared vision confidently.

Communication Styles

People's temperaments and communication styles vary, but some general observations can be made. When stressed or dealing with conflict, individuals often exhibit different tendencies. Recognizing these differences and allowing each other to express desires and fears in a safe environment is a good starting point for discussing important or sensitive topics.

Flow-oriented people tend to express interest in various subjects, speak quickly, and trust their instincts. They may say things impulsively and directly, often not worrying about social niceties. Flow people are good at energizing others and acting swiftly to achieve results. They excel as creative problem solvers but may avoid confrontation and rely on emotional responses instead of logic.

On the opposite end, certain communication styles prioritize privacy and look externally for data that confirms their conclusions. These individuals are concerned with adhering to rules and distinguishing between right and wrong.

Role Expectations

Every individual enters a marital relationship with specific role expectations. A frank discussion can help clarify these expectations and find a meeting point. Traditionally, men have expected women to manage the home. However, with the evolution of the family into the "nuclear family," these patriarchal expectations have changed. Women are now often expected to contribute financially as well.

Despite financial contributions, many women find their decision-making power limited. Their earnings are frequently allocated to domestic activities, while the remaining savings are controlled by their partners. Reflecting on the roles each partner plays in a marital relationship can reveal any evolved patterns and the balance of financial responsibilities. Financial contributions should be viewed as a partnership, with both partners having equal say in money management.

Marriage should be seen as a contract where roles and expectations evolve over time. Open discussions about role satisfaction are crucial, especially as family roles and worldviews continue to change.

CHAPTER 4

Navigating Difficult Conversations

Relationships are not solely about comfort and laughter. Sharing deep aspects of your inner world means learning how to navigate through the rough patches as well. Inevitably, difficult topics will arise during the marriage conversation. So, what should you do during those times?

What You Can Do:

Having preset strategies for handling difficult moments is always a great idea. When the tension is high between you and your partner, focus on addressing the problem, not the person. Often, the issue isn't the subject of the argument, but the manner in which the discussion is conducted.

Conflict Resolution Basics:

1. **Take Breaks:** If arguments start to build intensity, it's wise to take a break before emotions escalate. Taking a break is not about avoiding the issue but reducing the intensity to prevent a heated argument. Think of it as preventing the oils from hitting flashpoint—you don't want to ignite an inferno.

2. **Active Listening:** Active listening is crucial in relationships. It doesn't matter if someone can't speak your language; giving them attention and truly listening can communicate a lot. Listen without trying to solve the problem immediately; sometimes, just listening and acknowledging can make a significant difference. As the saying goes, "A problem shared is a problem halved."

3. **Manage Emotions:** Be aware of your own emotions and try to regulate them. If you escalate the conflict, your partner will likely escalate it too. Aim to be the one who takes a break or speaks gently, helping to de-escalate the situation.

4. **Seek Therapy Help:** Relationships can get complicated, and sometimes it's beneficial to seek professional help. A therapist can provide valuable insights and help both partners navigate through challenging times. Consider seeing a therapist before marriage, as it can lead to deeper conversations and stronger commitment. Counseling can intensify positive feelings and help address potential issues early on.

CHAPTER 5

Seeking Professional Help

If you're struggling to make up your mind about the marriage talk or can't seem to start a productive conversation with your partner, seeking professional help might be the next best step. Sitting down with a relationship expert—such as a marriage counselor, social worker, or psychologist—can provide valuable guidance and mediation. These professionals can help navigate the issues that have arisen due to marriage-related decisions and foster healthier communication between you and your partner.

Common Reasons for Seeking Relationship Counseling:

- **Problems with Communication:** If you find it challenging to hear your partner or feel misunderstood, a counselor can help both of you practice active listening and improve your communication skills. Effective communication is the cornerstone of any healthy relationship.
- **Issues with Sex and/or Sexuality:** Whether you're not enjoying sex, struggling with frequency, or feeling uncertain about your gender or sexuality, a "sexpert" can offer specialized guidance. Plan on consulting with two or three different professionals to find the one who best suits your needs and can help address your specific concerns.

- **Pre-Marital Counseling:** If you're already discussing marriage, pre-marital counseling can be beneficial. It allows you to learn more about your partner's values, ethics, and potential deal breakers before tying the knot. This proactive approach can pave the way for a stronger and more informed marital relationship.

CHAPTER 6

Moving Forward After the Marriage Talk

Assuming the marriage talk went well, you both feel clarity about where you stand, and you still want to continue building your relationship together, what are the next steps? If you know what you want, go get it! It's important to focus not only on the logistics, such as paperwork and ceremony planning but also on nurturing the emotional connection that brought you to this point. Celebrate milestones, show love and appreciation, and deepen your bond by sharing thoughts and plans for the future. While there's no magical formula for commitment, here are some steps to consider after the marriage talk:

- **Create a timeline**: Work through it together, making intentional plans and checking for discrepancies. Be patient and practice empathy, and don't hesitate to seek help when needed.

Life is rarely as straightforward as it seems. Complicated histories with other partners, careers, family, and children can add challenges.

Take the time to discuss these issues and get help when necessary. Marriage is not self-sustaining; it can fluctuate from exciting to challenging and back again. It requires determination and hard work.

Over the years, my wife and I have dedicated time to updating our relationship "plan" in a playful manner. We mark specific events we're excited about, care for each other, and evaluate our relationship's state.

Implementing Action Plans

The ideas formulated during the marriage talk should be put into action. Both partners should notice changes in the relationship and each other's behavior.

Changes could involve unofficial or casual long-term goals, such as sharing more about your lives, dreams, and ambitions. For example:

- "We shall attempt to spend at least 20 hours together each week, whether we can afford it or not."
- "Get up on time, even at 3:00 am, to speak to my partner when they need support."
- "Listen to their ideas and share my feelings more openly."

Goals should be specific and guide the direction of your efforts. Avoid vague statements like "We are going to work on our marriage." Be precise and actionable.

Revisiting and Reassessing

Regularly revisit and reassess the conclusions from the marriage talk. Perceptions and desires may change as you grow and learn more about each other. Periodically evaluating your relationship will help ensure it continues to progress positively. Consider reassessing your marriage talk every six, eight, or twelve months.

The conversation may also need to be revisited when key issues arise where you find yourselves differing in opinion. For instance, one partner might want to get married soon, while the other envisions a wedding in a few years. This dialogue may come up several times, especially if both partners continue to grow and feel comfortable in the relationship.

Conclusion

Transitioning into the "marriage phase" of a romantic relationship is a loving move, transforming the uncertainties of an important transition: "What are we doing?", "Where are we going?", and "What will it take to get there?". As we explore these questions, a new map of the relationship emerges, guiding us forward.

An ever-brilliant friend of mine regularly asks me to repeat my advice on the subject, so she can follow it herself. For the sake of the advice-column genre, I will add: Imagine my hand on the small of your back, gently guiding you back to your kitchen, away from the chaos. Seeking out these questions might indeed come at a cost.

Clarity is achieved. By its nature, the marriage talk compels potential partners to confront many questions with a blend of honesty and stakes that is rare outside of marriage. How do we handle conflict? What are the stakes? Do we truly love each other? Do our visions of the future intertwine?

If we weren't guided by this overarching narrative, would our love be as conscious? This revelation might make it easier for us to take the plunge, or harder. It's possible that with this newfound clarity, we might respond with kindness or cruelty we didn't know we had in us. It's hard to predict. But you might experience a lot by finding out.

9 798348 430474